To:

_____

From:

_____

Date:

_____

Devotions for Little Hearts

Discover the blessings in God's wonderful world

Wendy Maartens
Illustrated by Natalie & Tamsin Hinrichsin

christian
art kids

Copyright © 2015 by Christian Art Kids,
an imprint of Christian Art Publishers,
PO Box 1599, Vereeniging, 1930, RSA

359 Longview Drive, Bloomingdale, IL 60108, USA

First edition 2015

Translated from the Afrikaans
Dagstukkies vir klein hartjies
by Annegreth Rautenbach

Scripture quotations are taken from the Holy Bible, New Living
Translation® 1996, 2004, 2007, 2013 by Tyndale House Foundation.
Used by permission of Tyndale House Publishers Inc., Carol Stream, Illinois 60188.
All rights reserved.

Scripture quotations are taken from the Contemporary English Version®.
Copyright © 1995 by American Bible Society.
All rights reserved.

Scripture quotations are taken from the *Holy Bible*, New International Version®
NIV®. Copyright © 1973, 1978, 1984 by International Bible Society. Used by
permission of Zondervan Publishing House.
All rights reserved.

Scripture quotations are taken from the New King James Version.
Copyright © 1979, 1980, 1982 by Thomas Nelson, Inc. Used by permission.
All rights reserved.

Printed in China

ISBN 978-1-4321-2262-1

15 16 17 18 19 20 21 22 23 24 – 10 9 8 7 6 5 4 3 2 1

Contents

Introduction

Dear Parents and Caregivers,

We all know those precious moments when a child sees a ray of sunshine on their skin for the first time. Or the joy that a small bug, leaf or feather can give to a precious little one. For that reason, this devotional focuses specifically on nature and seasons, to instill those memorable lessons of faith in their hearts.

Each devotion consists of the following:

- an opening Scripture verse that introduces little ones to the Bible.
- **Something to Think About:** a short summary of the lesson for the day.
- **Prayer:** a short talk with God.
- **Something to Do:** a fun activity providing children the opportunity to apply what they've learned in a practical way.

You really only need 20 minutes a day to establish a precious quiet time with your child. A child who associates this kind of nurturing with bedtime has an added advantage for their emotional, social and mental development. But the most important bonus is that the child's journey of discovery includes an almighty, loving and creative God who never ceases to amaze and surprise us. And we can know with certainty that our child will slowly master the great and unfathomable world out there one step at a time, because they follow in God's caring footsteps!

Bear the following in mind:

- The intimate time spent between you and your child during your quiet times creates a feeling of fellowship and belonging. It gives your child the confidence to ask questions and talk about certain topics they may not do otherwise. So prepare yourself for an adventure!

- Don't rush. Relax and try to put the day's worries aside for a while. Your little one is a fine observer and will quickly see when your attention and focus are elsewhere.

- You don't need to read the devotions in chronological order. If your child needs to apologize to someone, read the piece about saying sorry. Look for ways to apply the stories to everyday situations.

- You and your child's time together is personal. It's the first building blocks of a lifelong relationship of trust. Respect their privacy, no matter how small they are. Keep the things that your child shares with you during this special time to yourself, no matter how sweet.

- The prayers are only guidelines. You can read them and give your child an opportunity to end with "Amen". Allow them to add a sentence or two or repeat your words. It's up to them. If they choose only to listen, that's also fine.

- Help your child to understand that God is always available, anytime of the day or night, not only during quiet time. And He always listens when we talk to Him! Encourage your child to tell

God about everything that bothers them or if there are things they wonder about.

- **Something to Do** gives your toddler the opportunity to experience the devotion with their senses and to really make the content practical. Encourage your child to use their imagination and to ask from an early age, "What would Jesus do?" A child who can think creatively won't back down from the challenges of life.
- There are devotions included for special days like birthdays, Easter, Ascension Day and Christmas. Adapt your bedtime routine on these days. Invite cousins, friends and visiting family on those days to join you.
- The devotions speak of a family setup with Dad, Mom, brothers and sisters. Adapt the characters to suit your setup or situation as caregiver.
- Assure your child on a regular basis of your love, but also of God's love for His children. Read Matthew 19:14 to your child: "Let the children come to Me. Don't stop them! For the Kingdom of Heaven belongs to those who are like these children."

Enjoy your reading and cuddling time! And don't forget to find the mouse hiding in every devotion!

Be a Ray of Sunshine!

God made two great lights – the larger one to govern
the day, and the smaller one to govern the night.
Genesis 1:16

God made the sun for us. It's like a big light bulb.
During the day it shines brightly so that we can see.
During the night it is dark so we can sleep tight.

In summertime the sun is extra hot. Then we have
picnics on the beach. Mom and Dad sit under the
colorful beach umbrella. We eat ice cream. Mom puts
sun screen lotion on my face. She says, "Remember to
wear your sun hat."

We collect sea shells and play in the water. Sometimes I
stay in the water until I begin to shiver. Then I lie on my
towel and bask in the sun.

Sometimes Dad swims with me and we run and jump
over the waves. We count, "One, two, three …
jump!" When there is a really big wave coming, Dad lifts
me onto his shoulders. We laugh a lot. Dad gives me
a hug. He says I'm his ray of sunshine!

God is our heavenly Dad. He loves us very much.
His love for us shines warm and bright like the sun.
        He wants us to be His sunshine children.

Something to Do

Ask Mom to draw a sun in the palm of your hand with her finger. Does it tickle? Now draw one with your finger on her palm.

Something to Think About

God's love feels just as nice as sunny weather.

Prayer

Jesus, I want to be Your sunshine child. Amen.

Slide on the Rainbow!

"I have placed My rainbow in the clouds."
Genesis 9:13

A rainbow is BIG and SO beautiful, just like a huge ribbon that God put in the sky. Do you also sometimes wish you could catch the rainbow? Then you could play on its colorful back. Or use it as a slide. Or a big tent!

Every rainbow is special. Look carefully. A rainbow only appears after rainy weather. After a big storm, you can see many rainbows in the sky. Without words a rainbow says, "Look, the clouds are disappearing. The sun is on its way!" Its bright colors say, "All the bad things are over. Only good things are coming!"

God created the first rainbow a long time ago. It was a special gift. God made it for Noah. It was a promise from God that He would never again send a flood to destroy the earth.

Every time Noah saw the rainbow, he knew that God always keeps His promises. Every time we see a rainbow, it is a reminder that God still keeps His promises. Not only to Noah, but also to you and me!

Something to Think About

God always keeps His promises.

Something to Do

How many colors of the rainbow can you name?

Prayer

Jesus, thank You for sending a rainbow after every storm.

Amen.

Plant a
Flower Garden

Flowers appear on the earth,
the season of singing has come.
Song of Solomon 2:12

We sleep more during wintertime than in summer. And it is nice to curl up under a soft blanket in rainy weather, especially when Mom reads a story!

Some animals, like the black bear, sleep the whole winter long. They only wake up again in spring.

Did you know that some plants also sleep during winter? Their bulbs lie quietly under the chilly ground. Flower bulbs have such pretty names, like lilies, anemones and orchids. They wait for the first rain to fall. They wait for the sun to shine nice and warm. They are not in a hurry. They know that springtime will come at just the right time.

Suddenly a little green leaf from the bulb will appear above the ground. And another one and another one. And then the flowers appear. Before you know it, the fields look like a flower garden!

We are also like flower bulbs. God planted wonderful bulbs deep in our hearts. Bulbs need love, obedience and honesty. Every time you do something good, one of the bulbs starts to bloom. And before long your heart will bloom like a colorful flower garden: God's flower garden!

Something to Do

Give someone a big hug today. Can you feel how your flower garden for God is growing?

Something to Think About

Do good things for other people and see how God's flower garden grows in your heart.

Prayer

Jesus, help me to be a beautiful flower garden for You.

Amen.

Don't Get Lost

A mist went up from the
earth and watered the
whole face of the ground.
Genesis 2:6

During winter, the mornings are sometimes foggy. It is easy to get lost in heavy fog, because you cannot see the road clearly. To drive in thick mist is even more dangerous. Mom or Dad must switch on the car's fog lights and drive really slowly. If you were sailing on the sea, you wouldn't be able to see the shore. The boat could crash against the rocks and sink!

Fortunately, there is a lighthouse. It shows the ships and boats where the dangerous rocks are. The light of the lighthouse flashes all the time. Without saying a word the light is saying, "Look at me and you will be safe."

Sometimes it is very difficult to do the right things. We get lost between being good and being naughty. Then God is our Lighthouse. He says, "Do all the things that I teach you. Then you will see My light flashing. You will be safe and you will make good choices."

Something to Do

Take a flashlight and switch it on when it's dark outside. Can you see how far the light beam shines?

Something to Think About

God helps us so we don't get lost.

Prayer

Jesus, help me to always watch and follow Your bright light.

Amen.

23

Snug beneath Mother Hen's Wings

"How often I have wanted to gather your children together as a hen protects her chicks beneath her wings."
Matthew 23:37

When an icy wind starts to blow, Mother Hen gathers her chicks. She calls them, "Cluck-cluck, cluck-cluck!" The chicks stop fiddling in the grass. They run to Mother Hen. And they all nestle under her wings. She puffs her feathers to make enough space for everyone. No one will get cold or stay outside.

25

Every now and then the busiest little chick will peep out from under her feathers. He is curious to see what is going on outside. "You're going to catch a cold," says Mother Hen. She gently pushes the little one back beneath her wings.

"I love each one of you," says Mother Hen. She puts her head under her feathers. And then she and her chicks sleep safe and warm.

God is our Mother Hen. We are His chicks. He looks after us. He doesn't want us to wander around in the cold. He wants us to be safe beneath His wings. He wants to look after us and keep us warm, every single day!

Something to Think About

God wants to
take care of
you every day.

Something to Do

If you have a pet, always
make sure that they have
a warm place to sleep
and a clean blanket.

Prayer

Jesus, please keep
me safe under
Your wings.
Amen.

Busy like an Ant

Have you ever watched an ant?
Ants are always busy. Sometimes they
walk so fast you cannot even see their little legs.
Ants work hard all the time. Sometimes they are
more hardworking than people. Ants never go on
holiday. They only talk about work. But take
a moment and watch ants carefully.

One ant will never pass by another one without stopping. Then they talk about work!

Ants may be small, but they are very strong. They can carry pieces of food that are much bigger than they are. Ants are good at making plans. In summertime there is lots of food for ants. Then the ants gather extra food and keep it in their nests. When winter comes, the fields are empty and there is not enough food for all the ants. All their hard work was worth the effort.

God wants us to be just as hard working as the ants. When you help Mom with chores around the house, it makes God happy. Or when you pick up your toys without being told to. You can help your little sister to button her shirt or you can be obedient when Dad tells you to do something.

Doing things like this makes you a winner!

Something to Do

Make Mom happy and ask her if you can help her with extra chores.

Something to Think About

God wants you to be hard working.

Prayer

Dear Jesus, I want to be as hard working as an ant. Please help me.

Amen.

Vines Bear Fruit

Jesus says, "I am the vine; you are the branches."
John 15:5

When it is time for grapes to be picked, the farmer keeps his eye on the vineyard. He waits until the big bunches of grapes are ripe. Then he calls his farm workers. "Today is the day," he says.

While they are singing cheerful songs, the workers get to work. They cut off the bunches of grapes and put them into big baskets. Then they carry the full baskets on their shoulders to the wagons. The pile of grapes get bigger and bigger. A tractor tows the wagon to the cellar. At the cellar the farmer uses the grapes to make grape juice or wine.

Sometimes Mom buys us grapes at the store. Round, purple and juicy grapes that shine like Grandma's purple necklace. The farmer looks after his vineyard. He cuts off every branch that does not produce fruit.

Jesus says that He is the Vine. We are the branches that bear sweet bunches of grapes. If we stay close to Him, we will be safe and bear much fruit.

Something to Do

Draw a picture of a bunch of grapes. Write the names of your family members next to each grape. Stick it on the fridge for everyone to see.

Something to Think About

God wants you to stay close to Him and listen to Him.

Prayer

Jesus, I want to be a branch that bears sweet grapes for You.

Amen.

Every Snowflake Is Unique

He sends the snow
like white wool.
Psalm 147:16

In wintertime God sprinkles snow on the mountaintops. It sparkles in the light of the moon at night. Children can play in the snow and build snowmen. Each one thinks their snowman looks the best!

One little boy wants to take his snowman home. His mommy laughs, "No, honey, your snowman will melt! And only a puddle of water will be left."

It's amazing to watch the white snowflakes float from the sky, almost like small feathers. Did you know that if you look through a magnifying glass, each snowflake looks different? Each one has its own special pattern.

God made us just as wonderful. We are all made with a unique and special pattern. Some children are tall, and others are short. Some have black hair, and others are blonde or have red hair. Some kids have blue eyes, and others have brown or green eyes. Some children can run fast, and others can sing beautifully. Some kids are shy and others are not.

No one in the whole wide world is the same. Each one of us is special. Much more special than a snowflake!

Something to Do

Look at yourself in the mirror. You are precious. You are one of a kind!

Something to Think About

God makes each person special and unique.

Prayer

Dear Jesus, thank You that You made me so much more special than a snowflake! Amen.

Silly Wind!

Jesus calmed the
storm to a whisper.
Psalm 107:29

The wind can be really silly sometimes. It can pluck Grandma's hat from her head. It can blow your dress over your head. And it can mess up the cat's fur.

The wind can also be kind. It can dry the laundry. It can make your kite fly high up in the sky. And it can blow the sails of the boats on the sea.

But the wind can sometimes be rough too. A scary rushing wind that howls around the corners of the house. A wild gust of wind that blows roofs off and pulls trees over. A rough wind that makes big waves and turns boats upside-down.

We are not strong or clever enough to stop the wind. It blows wherever it wants. Only God is strong and clever enough to tell the wind, "No, naughty wind, enough is enough! When I speak, you must listen!"

Then the wind stops blowing trees over and roofs off houses. The wind doesn't make huge waves anymore and doesn't turn boats upside-down. It looks at all the things it has broken and feels very sorry.

"That is better," says God. "Settle down now."

Something to Do

Help Mom to hang the washing. Watch how it flaps in the wind.

Something to Think About

God is stronger than the wind.

Prayer

Dear Jesus, thank You that even the wind listens when You speak!

Amen.

Clouds Are Wonderful!

*The Lord went ahead of them. He guided
them during the day with a pillar of cloud.*
Exodus 13:21

If the weather is good, the clouds look soft and fluffy.
They look so nice to jump on ... almost like a jumping
castle.

Have you ever watched the clouds? Some clouds look
like a ship. Others look like a dog, or a duck. It is great to
watch the clouds change into new shapes all the time.

Clouds are wonderful things! They bring rain for plants

to grow. And they provide water for humans and animals. Without clouds we can't swim or bath. We can't cook or even boil the kettle.

When a storm is coming, clouds look angry. Then they make a lot of noise and lightening flashes. But it's all just bragging, because before long all the clouds disappear just like opening a curtain to let the sun in.

God makes every cloud. From the tiniest white cloud to the biggest, darkest thundercloud. He made a special cloud for the Israelites when they traveled through the desert. God said to them, "Follow this cloud, it will show you where to go."

Something to Do

Imagine you are floating on a cloud over your house. What do you see?

Something to Think About

God makes every single cloud so wonderful!

Prayer

Dear Jesus, thank You for making clouds that bring rain.

Amen.

Happy Birthday to You!

Lord, I will praise You
with songs.
Psalm 101:1

Today is my birthday! I counted down the days one by one. Mom helped me to cross them out with my crayon on the calendar. Now the day is here. I'm so excited! I quickly jump out of bed and change into my new clothes that Mom and Dad bought especially for my birthday.

The sun is peeping through the window. The sun says, "Good morning, Birthday Friend. You look smart!"

Kitty rubs against my legs. She turns and looks up at me. She says, "Happy Birrrrrthday! Happy Birrrrrthday!"

I run to Mom and Dad's bedroom. I jump on their bed and lie next to them. Mom takes my present out of the bedside drawer. I can't wait to open it. It's a Children's Bible with lots of pictures and big letters. "You are our greatest gift ever," says Mom. "Jesus gave you to us as a special gift," says Dad. Then they sing to me: "Happy Birthday, our dearest child!"

Something to Think About

You are a gift from God.

Something to Do

Do you know someone who doesn't have a mom or dad? Find out when their birthday is. Ask Mom to do something special for them on that day.

Prayer

Dear Jesus, birthdays are great! Thank You for them. Today is such fun!

Amen.

Rise and Shine!
It is a Beautiful Day!

*Both day and night
belong to You, Lord.*
Psalm 74:16

In summer the days are long. The sun rises early in the morning. While we are still fast asleep, Mister Sun peeps through the window. He says, "Rise and shine! It's a beautiful day! The birds are singing and the flowers are awake!"

There is more than enough time in summer to do all the things that you enjoy. It's hard to choose between swimming, riding your bike, playing hide and seek or swinging.

Wintertime is different. The days are shorter and the nights are long and cold. When the alarm clock goes off, nobody feels like getting up. We must switch on the light, because the sun only peeps through the window a bit later now. He also does not feel like rising. He wants to sleep in. Even the birds are quiet. Their heads are still buried under their wings.

The long days of summer and the short days of winter all belong to God. He sees to it that all the days follow after each other on the calendar, each in its own block. Just when we get tired of the same weather, God surprises us with a change in the season. And each season has its own joys!

Something to Do

Look at the calendar with Mom. Look for your birthday on the calendar. Is your birthday in summer or winter?

Something to Think About

God wants you to enjoy every single day.

Prayer

Dear Jesus, thank You for each brand-new day filled with joy and laughter. Amen.

55

Everything in Its Time

**For everything
there is a ... time.**
Ecclesiastes 3:1

Animals and plants don't wear watches. God created them to know when it is their time to do their jobs. God lets the thrush sing every morning at the same time. He tells the finches when it is springtime. Then they are hard at work building their nests and laying their eggs. He even tells the lizards when it is warm enough to come out from under the rocks.

God also tells the trees what to do. In autumn He gives

the leaves yellow and orange jackets to wear. During winter the bare branches rest. In spring it's time to show off! God gives every tree a pretty pink or white blossom dress!

God also keeps time for us. He wakes us up in the morning for the new day ahead. He gives us time for breakfast and to play with friends. He gives us time so our teacher can teach us new things at school. He also gives us time to watch TV, but not too much! When Mom and Dad are home from work, God gives family time. He wants us to sit together to eat, and talk and laugh and read the Bible!

God also gives us the best time of all — time for hugs!

Something to Think About

God lets everything happen at the right time.

Something to Do

Ask Mom to show you how to set the alarm clock for tomorrow morning.

Prayer

Jesus, thank You for holding the whole world's big clock in Your hands. Amen.

Rain, Rain, Beautiful Rain!

*You send rain on the mountains
from Your heavenly home.*
Psalm 104:13

Do you also love the sound
of rain against the window panes?
You watch the pitter-patter of the raindrops on the
ground. It is fun to blow against the window and watch
the vapor. I draw a heart on the window. Mom draws a
butterfly and my little sister draws a flower.

All the dust is washed from the leaves of the plants.
The flowers' bright dresses are extra shiny! Even the
grass looks washed clean.

The wagtails puff their feathers and bathe in the puddles.
The ducks play in the pond. The rivers flow strongly, and all
the old leaves and branches are washed away.

The sky seems more
blue after the rain.
The sun smiles!

God's forgiveness is like rain. It washes all the
bad things from our hearts. We do not need
to do anything in return. All we have to do is
say, "Sorry, God. Please forgive me."

You are so special to God that He does not
make you wait. He forgives you right away.
Even before you are finished talking, your
heart is cleaned. All the naughty things are
gone. Your light can now shine bright again.

Oh, I love the rain!

Something to Think About

God's forgiveness washes you clean like rain.

Something to Do

Next time it rains look out the window and see how God washes everything clean.

Prayer

Dear Jesus, I am sorry I was naughty. Please make my heart clean again. Amen.

I Am a Fruit Tree

> "A tree is identified by its fruit. Figs are never gathered from thornbushes, and grapes are not picked from bramble bushes."
>
> Luke 6:44

Do you also love oranges? They look like orange lights hanging on the trees. Dad always buys us oranges at the fruit shop. Then we make a hole in the top and suck the juice out. It is sweet, cool and delicious.

Grandma loves to buy apples. She gives me a red apple for my teacher. Grandma uses the green apples to make apple crumble. Yum!

Sometimes, Grandpa peels an apple for me with his pocketknife. He cuts the apple in slices. "One for me ... one for you," says Grandpa.

Healthy fruit trees give juicy fruit. They make the farmer's heart glad. We are glad if we can feast on the sweet fruits! God's heart is also glad.

We are God's fruit trees. He wants us to bear only good fruit. You can easily see which people bear good fruit. They are friendly and loving. They don't use bad words and they are patient. They do good things for others.

You are God's special child. You are His fruit tree, the most beautiful and best fruit tree in His garden!

Something to Think About

God's children bear good fruit.

Something to Do

Give a shiny red apple to the beggar at the street corner. Tell them, "God loves you."

Prayer

Jesus, I want to bear sweet and juicy fruit for You. Please help me. Amen.

Let Your Little Light Shine

Lord, You are my lamp.
2 Samuel 22:29

In winter it gets dark earlier. Dad switches on the lights of the car when he drives home after work. At home Mom switches on the lights because she needs to see clearly when she is making dinner. Grandma also needs light to knit a jersey for me. My big brother needs to switch on the light to do his homework. And I need the light to color in.

When the power goes out, I am a little scared. We cannot see in the dark. Everybody stumbles around. I don't like the dark, so I jump on Mom's lap. I just sit there for a while.

"Don't worry," says Dad and takes out matches to light the candles. He puts the candles on the table. "That is better!" laughs Mom. "See how the little light chases away the darkness?" We are all glad that the candle makes light. Light is friendly and warm, almost as if saying, "Come closer, come closer!"

You are God's light. It shines from deep within your heart. God put His light in you. When you are loving towards other people, your light burns brightly. It tells people to come closer. Come closer and feel God's kindness and love.

Something to Think About

God's love shines like a light inside your heart.

Something to Do

Do something kind for someone in your family. You are a light shining for Jesus!

Prayer

Dear Jesus, I want my light to tell others to come closer to You!
Amen.

I Like the Color Blue

The heavens declare the glory of God;
the skies proclaim the work of His hands.

Psalm 19:1

The blue sky is so beautiful! It looks like God paints it with a different brush every day, just for us! In summer the sky is almost as clear blue as the ocean. During winter the sky is pale blue, as if it is also getting cold. In the early evening God adds a little purple. Then the sun's rays look extra pretty. At night the sky is a dark blue so that we can see the stars shine bright.

Dad's eyes are also blue. Mom says they are even more blue when he laughs. The peacock on Uncle John's farm is blue. He displays his tail feathers to us. Every feather shines like a gemstone.

The cornflowers in Aunt Mary's garden are blue. When we visit her she always gives me a bunch to take home.

My shoes are blue. When I wear them I pretend to walk on the clouds.

But my new blue quilt is the prettiest. Grandma made it. She says every block is a love letter from her and Jesus, especially for me!

Something to Think About

God made the sky blue.

Something to Do

Look at the big blue sky and thank God for creating it.

Prayer

Dear Jesus, thank You for everything blue. I like it all so much!

Amen.

75

Angels around Us

*"I am sending an angel before you
to protect you on your journey."*
Exodus 23:20

God made the seasons. He cares for the sun, the moon and the stars. He cares for every animal, from the biggest elephant to the tiniest bird. Even if God has a lot of work to do, He never forgets about us.

Many years ago God sent an angel to Moses. The angel had to protect Moses and the people. He had to help them to not get lost. All God asked of Moses and the people were for them to obey Him.

God sends angels to protect people. We cannot see angels, but we know they are around us.

Angels obey God and do what He tells them. In the Bible we read of angels who came to earth as God's messengers. An angel visited Mary to tell her she would have a baby, His name would be Jesus.

In heaven the angels worship God. In the Bible we read about how the angels sing and praise God.

The angels also rejoice over every person who accepts Jesus into their hearts.

Just think, one day in heaven you can join in the angels' songs of praise to God!

Something to Do:

Look at your own shadow. Can you run away from it? Angels are as close to us as our very own shadow.

Something to Think About

God sends angels to protect us.

Prayer

Dear Jesus, thank You for angels who look after us.

Amen.

Hide and Seek

**My God is the mighty
rock where I hide.**

Psalm 94:22

Have you ever seen or watched a rock hyrax (dassie)
high up in the mountains? They are cute and furry,
right? They have no tail and their noses are shiny.
During the day they like to bask in the sun. Each family
huddles together. Grandma and Grandpa help Mom and
Dad. They all keep an eye on the busy little ones.

Suddenly there is a strange noise. In a flash they all
hide in the cleft of the rock. Not even one shiny
nose can be seen. Now the eagle can come.
He won't be able to get at any rock
hyrax from under the rock. The
jackal will also not find them.

The rock is their safe hiding place. Nobody can harm them while they are hiding in the rock crevice.

We are sometimes like the dassie. We get scared quickly. Fortunately, we have a Rock where we can hide, a huge Rock where no one can find you. Not even your little toe sticks out when you hide there. There is space for all the people that you love, even your kitty cat and your hamster.

The name of the Rock is God. He is solid like a mountain. You can hide with Him whenever you want!

Something to Do

Imagine that you are a dassie and that an eagle is chasing you. Hide quickly under your bed. Whew, that feels better! In the same way, you can hide with God.

Something to Think About

God is a safe hiding place.

Prayer

Dear Jesus, I want to hide with You just like a dassie hides in the rocks for safety.
Amen.

The Little Lamb

He will carry the lambs in His arms,
holding them close to His heart.
Isaiah 40:11

A shepherd loves his sheep. He knows every single one.
He knows which one always wants to walk in front.
He also knows which ones like to chase butterflies, or
which little lamb is scared of a big, bad wolf.

Early in the morning the shepherd
leads his sheep out of the pen. Then
they walk to the field. The sheep know
his voice. When he calls them, they
follow. Sometimes the shepherd sings.
The sheep like it a lot. They leap for joy
behind him.

The shepherd protects his sheep against wild animals. When a lamb is too tired, the shepherd carries them. If a lamb gets sick, the shepherd takes them home to care for them.

God is our Shepherd. We are His sheep. He knows each one of us. He knows who likes ice cream and who does not like veggies. He knows who is afraid of the dark and who likes to collect sea shells.

God wants to be with us all the time. Just like a shepherd looks after his sheep, He wants to protect us from harm. He wants to carry us when we get tired. He wants to care for us when we are sick. We just need to stay close to Him.

Something to Do

Hold your one hand up. Say: "The Lord is my Shepherd." Count down each word on your fingers. Now do the same with your toes.

Something to Think About

God is your Shepherd.

Prayer

Dear Jesus, I want to be one of Your sheep. Hold me close to Your heart.
Amen.

It Is Easter

*"He isn't here! He is
risen from the dead."*
Matthew 28:6

Jesus had a very important
mission on earth. He had to die on
a cross to pay for our sins. Even
though Jesus wanted to do this,
He was still scared. God sent an
angel to comfort Him.

A group of soldiers came to arrest Jesus. All His friends ran away. The soldiers made fun of Jesus and hurt Him. Jesus did not fight back. The soldiers were very surprised. *This is a very special person,* they thought.

Jesus did not do anything wrong, but He was still taken to court. Some people told lies about Him. Jesus did not say anything. He just kept quiet.

The judge sent Jesus to be crucified. They put a crown of thorns on His head and He was nailed to a cross. Jesus felt very sad and alone. But He did not think about Himself. He prayed for the people who had hurt Him.

At twelve o'clock that day it suddenly became pitch dark. Jesus called out, "Father, I'm coming to You now!" Then He died. Jesus was wrapped in linen cloth and buried in a tomb.

On the Sunday morning, Jesus' friends went to visit the tomb. Jesus' body was not there anymore. He was raised from the dead, just like He promised!

Something to Think About

Jesus is stronger than death.

Something to Do

When one of your friends is mean to you, try to be like Jesus. Do something nice for him or her.

Prayer

Dear Jesus, You paid a high price for my sins. Thank You! I don't want to be naughty ever again. Amen.

Your Name Is Written on the Palms of God's Hands

"See, I have written your name on the palms of My hands."
Isaiah 49:16

Each tree has a name. So does every flower, bug and bird. Some have very funny names, like willie wagtail, sausage tree, kiss-me-over-the-garden-gate, or monkey puzzle tree. Some are difficult to say — real tongue twisters.

Each day of the week also has a name. You know them, right? Monday, Tuesday, Wednesday …

Towns and cities also have names. Some towns have silly names like Pie Town, Smileyberg, Oddville and Cheesequake.

A name tells a whole story. Moms and Dads think long and hard before they choose a name for their babies. They want it to sound nice, and mean something special.

Did you know? Even long before you were born, God knew your name! He knew exactly what you would look like. And He has loved you ever since. He loves you so much that your name is written on the palms of His hands.

It doesn't matter how naughty you have been. God will never love you less. Your name cannot be washed from His hands. It is written there forever and ever!

Something to Do

Whom do you love very, very much? Ask someone to write that person's name on the palm of your hand.

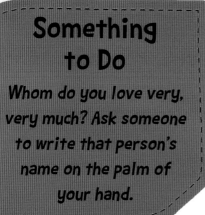

Something to Think About

God knows your name.

Prayer

Dear Jesus, thank You for never washing my name off Your hands!

Amen.

No More Desert!

Some wandered in the
wilderness, lost and homeless.
Psalm 107:4

When it does not rain, the plants wilt. The flowers die and fall off. The field turns brown and dull. The trees stop bearing fruit. The birds and butterflies fly away. The mice and squirrels look for other places to stay. Even the tortoise packs up and leaves. "It is too hard to stay here," he says.

All that is left is a desert with sand and rocks. A warm, dry wind blows over the field. It sounds as if nature is crying.

A joyful person can also turn into a wilderness. When other people are always mean to you, you can wilt. If you feel sad every day, your flowers will die and fall off. Naughty things can make your heart just as dull as the field without rain. Your smile disappears. And your cheerful songs find a new place to stay. Even the love in your heart packs up and leaves. Your heart becomes like a desert.

But God always sends rain, also in our hearts. Our wilted leaves turn green again. Here and there new flowers start to bloom. We smile and our songs return. God's love finds a way into our hearts again. He always gives new life!

Something to Think About

God gives new life. He makes our hearts blossom with His love.

Something to Do

Ask Mom for a flat container. Pour water into it. Put it outside and watch the birds drink from it.

Prayer

Dear Jesus, please make my heart brand new with Your new life!
Amen.

Flap Your Wings

**The wings of the
ostrich flap joyfully.**
Job 39:13

"All things bright and beautiful, all creatures great and small, all things wise and wonderful, the Lord God made them all." This is a happy song about nature.

To play outside makes one feel happy and joyful. Because what can be more fun than to play around in a heap of autumn leaves? Or to watch the blossoms float down

from the trees like confetti? Do you like to play in the rain or snow? All these fun things to do outside in nature makes your heart sing!

Animals can also be joyful. Watch how excited your puppy gets when he runs outside. He chases his own tail and jumps through the air!

Listen to the cheerful sounds of the birds in the garden. It's almost as if they are having a party. Even Mother Ostrich happily flaps her wings and runs in circles through the field. The baby ostriches follow her around. They play follow-the-leader.

God wants us to be happy and joyful. He has a special place in His heart for children. Let's sing a happy song — just for Him!

Something to Think About

God wants you
to be happy.

Something to Do

Pretend to be an ostrich.
Run around and flap your
wings. Sing a cheerful song
while you do it.

Prayer
Dear Jesus, help me to be
like a cheerful little
ostrich for You!
Amen.

Do You Want to Be My Friend?

They entered the boat in pairs, male and female, just as God had commanded Noah.

Genesis 7:9

In the beginning, God made Adam. He was the first person on earth. But he was lonely and sad! Then God made a friend for him. Adam was very happy. He had someone to talk to. Eve picked flowers with him and helped him to care for the animals. They had fun together. They lay next to each other on the grass and counted the stars. That was great!

God cared for Adam, but He also looked after the animals, fish and birds. Each animal had the perfect mate. They were like two peas in a pod. The gigantic whale got a friend just as big as him. The two of them could dive through the waves together.

The tiny ladybug got the same tiny friend. They sat together on a flower and swayed in the summer breeze.

Birds also have special songs they use to call each other.

God doesn't want us to be lonely. He wants us to have friends so that we can play and laugh together. And someone to hold our hand when we are sad or scared. God has the perfect friend for you.

Something to Do

Do you know someone who is lonely? Go to that person. Smile and ask them to be your friend.

Prayer

Dear Jesus, I know You have the perfect friend for me. Please send that friend my way.

Amen.

107

Ready, Steady, Go!

"Now learn a lesson from the fig tree. When its branches bud and its leaves begin to sprout, you know that summer is near."
Matthew 24:32

A fig tree is a wonderful thing! Its huge leaves look like hands waving in the wind. Its trunk is gray and smooth, perfect for climbing. The shade of the tree is nice and cool on a hot day. You can play with your dolls or read a book in its shade. And figs are the yummiest fruit. You can sit high up in the tree and enjoy the juicy figs!

Grandma makes jam from the fruit, while Mom bakes a pie. And I love to eat the fig syrup. Even the sparrows get their share.

After all the hustle and bustle, the fig tree becomes tired. Its leaves turn yellow and fall off. Its branches rest during the winter. The tree will need its strength to grow new green leaves and juicy figs. God prepares the fig tree for spring.

We are like fig trees. At night we sleep so we can rest, because we need our strength to work hard and do good things for others. God makes us strong so that we can work for Him. "Ready, steady ... go!"

Something to Think About

God makes us strong.

Something to Do

Ask Mom to call out:
"Ready, steady, go!"
And run like a champion!
Because you are one!

Prayer

Dear Jesus, make me
strong and bright to work
for You today.
Amen.

Can You Guess the Answer?

"The very hairs on your head are all numbered."
Luke 12:7

Have you ever tried to count the hairs on your head? Or the little curls on your dog's tail? Rather try to count Kitty's whiskers. Or the scales on your goldfish.

This is not so easy, right? There are so many that you forget halfway through. And it is far too hard to guess the answer.

I know Someone who knows exactly how many hairs are on your head. He knows how many curls are on your dog's tail. And how many whiskers Kitty has! In fact, He knows how many hairs are on the heads of all the people in the whole world!

His name is God. He loves us very much. He loves us so much that He knows everything about us. He knows how many leaves are on every tree. And He knows how many stars are in the sky. He even counts all the grains of sand on the beach.

God does not want us to be scared when we don't know something. We can ask Him. He knows anything and everything. He is waiting to help us!

Something to Do

Pick up a small leaf and let Mom guess which hand it is hidden in. If she guesses the right answer, it's her turn to hide something in her hand.

Something to Think About

God knows everything.

Prayer

Dear Jesus, You know the answers to all the questions. You are so great! Thank You for always helping me. Amen.

A Bubbling Fountain

You make springs pour water into the ravines,
so streams gush down from the mountains.

Psalm 104:10

A fountain is awesome. The water bubbles up from deep below the ground. Fountain water is clear and refreshing. It gives life to all things. Plants and flowers grow around a fountain. The soft moss makes comfy seats for butterflies and dragonflies. Birds make their nests in the trees around a fountain. They sing joyful songs. They know they never have to look for water.

They will never become thirsty. The fountain gives water in summer and winter. There is always enough for everyone.

All the wild animals visit the fountain. The deer drinks the water quietly. The warthogs lap the water daintily. Elephants use their trunks and giraffes must bend their long necks to take a sip!

Inside me there is also a fountain. It comes from deep inside my heart. My fountain of love is a nice place to be for the people around me. Grown-ups want to talk with me, and friends want to play with me. Even Kitty wants to sit on my lap to get a hug from me!

Something to Do

Do you know of an elderly person who is lonely? Ask them to tell you a story. Remember to thank them.

Something to Think About

God's fountain of love flows in your heart.

Prayer

Dear Jesus, I want my love for You and others to flow from my heart.
Amen.

Thank You for Another Day

The sun knows when to set.

Psalm 104:19

The sun is so clever! It knows exactly when to rise each morning. And it never forgets. No one has to tell the sun to start shining. It does it on its own. He peeks from behind the mountain or peers through the window, always with a big golden smile!

All day long he watches us from his house high up in the sky. He walks along his path through the blue sky every day. In the afternoon his shadow becomes tall. It is time to say goodbye.

The sky turns orange and yellow. The sun looks like a big golden ball that slowly sets on the horizon.

Then it is time to pack away my toys. It is almost time to bath and eat dinner. Before I go to sleep Mom reads me a bedtime story. When the story is finished, she kisses me on the cheek. She tucks me in and turns off the light.

One, two, three. My light and the sun's light is out!

God gives us a new day every day, just like He does for the sun! I also want to shine bright with a big golden smile. Just for Him!

Something to Do

Draw a big yellow sun. Then draw a big smile on its face. Stick it to your bedroom wall. Remember every day to wear your smile as you wear your clothes.

Something to Think About

God makes every brand-new day.

Prayer

Dear Jesus, thank You for giving me a gift every single day – a new day!
Amen.

High up in My Watchtower

I will climb up to my watchtower
and stand at my guardpost.
Habakkuk 2:1

Have you ever stood high up on a mountain?
Everything down below looks so small.
The houses and cars look like toys. It seems
like you can scrape together the rivers and
cars with one hand. Sometimes you can see
the ocean. The big waves rolling onto the
beach. It looks like you can blow the boats
over. You feel big and strong, like a giant
from a storybook.

A tree is also a good place for a watchtower. Especially when you have a tree house. Then you can see everything that happens on the ground. You can see if someone is coming. You feel rather important, like a king sitting on his throne.

This wonderful feeling does not last forever. Sometimes the world seems very, very big and you feel very, very small. So small that you just want to hide. Then you must ask God to be your Watchtower. He sees much farther than when you sit in a tree or stand on a mountaintop. His watchtower is heaven. From there He can watch over the whole earth. He watches over you every day with a heart filled with love.

Something to Do

Ask a grown-up to take you to the park. Swing as high as you can. Touch the sky with your toes. God is greater than the sky or the earth.

Something to Think About

God watches over me every minute of every day and night.

Prayer

Jesus, the world is so big and I feel very small. Thank You for watching over me.

Amen.

Jesus Goes Back to Heaven

He was taken up into a cloud while they were watching, and they could no longer see Him.
Acts 1:9

After Jesus was raised from the dead, He was on earth for a little while longer. Everybody knew that Jesus was King! He was greater than even death. His work on earth was done. He could return to His Father in heaven.

One day Jesus was walking with His disciples. He told them, "Go and wait in Jerusalem. God is going to send you a Helper."

The disciples were very curious. They asked all kinds of questions. But Jesus said, "Only God, the Father, knows when things will happen. But do not worry. He will give you strength. He will help you to tell other people about Me. You must also baptize them and teach them about Me."

Then a big cloud took Jesus up to heaven.

Two angels in white clothes appeared. "Do not be sad," they said. "Jesus will one day come back on the clouds."

The disciples wiped away their tears. Jesus was gone. But not forever. He would return again to fetch His children.

Something to Think About

Jesus will come back to earth one day to take His children back to heaven with Him.

Something to Do

Lie on your back on the grass. Look at the clouds. Jesus will come again on the clouds.

Prayer

Dear Jesus, I know You are coming back on the clouds to take me with You to heaven. Amen.

Always One More Chance

*Even a tree has more
hope! If it is cut down,
it will sprout again.*
Job 14:7

It is sad when a tree is cut down, because a tree gives shade and oxygen so we can breathe. It gives fruit and flowers. It gives birds a place to build a nest. And you can climb in it.

But there is always new hope. It is not long before a new green bud appears on the trunk. It opens up little leaves as if everyone is saying, "Yay! A second chance!"

Sometimes you feel like a tree that has been cut down. You do something wrong and you get into trouble. Dad is mad and Mom is very disappointed. Your friends do not want to play with you. You want to hide in the closet and never come out.

Thankfully there is always hope! God never forgets about you. He sees you, even when you are hiding in the dark closet. He is not mad at you. He knows you and He loves you even more than your mom and dad ever can. He wants to give you a second chance.

It won't be long before you feel so much better! You will tell everyone, "Yay, God gave me another chance. I can start over!"

Something to Do

Play tag with your friend. When your friend's turn is up, give them a brand-new turn. That is what God is doing for you every day!

Something to Think About

God always gives second chances.

Prayer

Dear Jesus, thank You for always giving me another chance.

Amen.

Stop the Fire!

*A tiny spark can set
a great forest on fire.*
James 3:5

A wildfire can be a terrible thing.
It crackles and creaks like an angry
dragon. You can feel its hot breath from
far away. His flames devour everything.
Everyone must flee, from the tiniest bug to
the tallest giraffe. And what about the tortoise
with his bandy legs? And the chameleon that
wants to swing on the tree branch?

That is why we should not
play with matches
or fire.

137

That is why grown-ups should not throw their cigarette butts out the car window. One tiny spark can set a whole forest on fire.

Your tongue can also be like a wildfire. Even if the tongue is so small, it can cause big trouble. One wrong word can cause a big fight. And one ugly remark can break someone's heart. One lie can lead to your friends not wanting to play with you anymore.

God wants us to watch what we say, like a police officer who must stop bad words. God wants you to think before you speak.

Let your words be like cool water that puts out a wildfire.

Something to Do

Count to ten and keep your mouth shut. That is the best way to keep your tongue from hurting others.

Something to Think About

God wants you to watch what you say.

Prayer

Dear Jesus, let my words be cool water that can put out any fire.
Amen.

Wait a Minute

Consider the farmers who
patiently wait for the rains
in the fall and in the spring.
James 5:7

A farmer is good at being patient. First, he has to wait for the right season. Then he can plow the land and sow the grain. Then he must wait for the rain. Then he waits for the seeds to grow. He watches them every day. He waits for the precious wheat to ripen and for the right time to harvest. A farmer never becomes tired of waiting. He knows that everything happens at the right time. Not sooner and not later. Waiting is always worth it.

Every day we need to wait for things.
You are excited to count down
the days to your next birthday or
Christmas. Or to wait for Grandpa
and Grandma to come visit. But to
wait for your food when you are
very hungry is more difficult.
And to wait your turn to speak
is also not easy.

God wants us to learn to
wait and be patient, even
if it is really hard. He lets
everything happen at
exactly the right time.
If we can learn to be
patient, every day
will feel like your
birthday!

Something to Think About

God wants you to be able to wait and be patient.

Something to Do

Ask Mom to put her finger over her mouth every time you interrupt her. Then you will remember to wait for her to finish talking first.

Prayer

Dear Jesus, it is not easy to wait. Please help me be better at waiting.

Amen.

Thank You

*He fell to the ground at
Jesus' feet, thanking Him.*
Luke 17:16

Moms do their best to teach their children good manners. To say thank you is very important.

Long ago the people had to carry rocks to a certain place to thank God. They used the rocks to build an altar. On the altar they brought their offerings. Poor people brought two or three doves as their offering. Rich people brought a sheep or a goat. Fortunately, we do not have to carry rocks anymore to thank God. We can talk to Him like we talk to a friend. We do not need a phone.

We can thank Him any time of the day or night. He is always there to listen.

Thank you is a golden word. God loves those words. It makes His heart glad.

You can sing it to Him. You can do a thank You dance or do three somersaults. You can pick up sea shells or a feather for Him. You can even wear your Sunday dress to thank Him. As long as you use the golden words wherever you go.

Something to Think About

God wants you
to say thank you.

Something to Do

Ask Mom to help you write
down the golden words. Write
them with your finger in the
sand. Pick a flower and put it
next to the words.

Prayer

Dear Jesus, I really want to
remember to say thank you.
Especially to You.
Amen.

The Brave Mouse

**Even when I walk
through the darkest
valley, I will not be afraid.**
Psalm 23:4

Once upon a time there was a
mouse. He was the king of the house.
During the day he marched up and
down singing: *"I'm a brave, brave
mouse. I go marching through the
house. And I'm not afraid of anything."*

But just wait until nighttime. Then he is
scared of all the dark corners in the house.
And he is scared of a trap, and a cat and a
man. He is scared of things that can catch
him. His mouth and his whiskers tremble.
Gone is the brave mouse from the day time!

Are you also scared at night? Are you scared of the long, dark passage? Or are you scared about something you saw on TV? Or something your friend told you about?

God doesn't want us to be scared. He loves us. He wants to protect us and care for us, like only He can. All we have to do is to obey Him and give Him a place in our hearts and home.

You are God's child. You can sing every day, "I'm a brave, brave mouse. I go marching through the house."

Something to Do

March round the house. Sing as loud as you can, "I'm a brave, brave mouse. God lives in our house. And I'm not afraid of anything!"

Something to Think About

God does not want you to be scared.

Prayer

Dear Jesus, thank You that I don't need to be scared of anything because You are with us.

Amen.

God's Firefly

The angel of the Lord appeared to him in a blazing fire from the middle of a bush.

Exodus 3:2

Moses was busy looking after his sheep. Everything was quiet. It was just him and his sheep in the wilderness. Suddenly a bush started to burn. Moses stepped closer. Then he heard a voice from the flames. It was God speaking, "Moses! Moses!"

"Here I am," Moses replied. From that day on, God's fire burned in Moses' heart. It made him strong and wise. It helped him to free the Israelites from Egypt. Not even the mighty pharaoh could stop him!

We know different types of fire: candles burning on a birthday cake, fireworks and the fireplace. But nothing is as strong and wonderful as God's fire. It is called the Holy Spirit. The Holy Spirit burns inside the hearts of all God's children.

You can see if God's fire is in someone's heart. That person is obedient, patient and loving.

If you have the flame of God's love in your heart, nothing can blow it out. It is yours to burn brightly, like a joyful firefly.

Prayer

Dear Jesus, I want to be Your firefly! Amen.

Something to Do

Put your hand where your heart is. Can you feel it beating? God's flame is also burning inside you.

Something to Think About

God's flame burns in your heart.

155

A Peaceful Heart

He leads me beside
peaceful streams.
Psalm 23:2

We are having a picnic by the lake. The water rushes
past like a wide shiny ribbon. It splashes peacefully over
the rocks. If I sit really still, I can see the fish swim at
the bottom of the lake.

We do fun things by the lake. Dad catches fish. My big brother
plays with his boat. I collect round pebbles. They all fit into
my bucket. Mom sits on the blanket and reads her

book. She watches the dragonflies' shiny blue wings.

When we spend time by the lake we feel relaxed. Our hearts are filled with peace. We forget to shout or fight.

I pick up a special pebble and give it to Mom. She smiles and hugs me tight.

We can't have a picnic by the lake every day. But God wants us to carry a river of peace in our hearts every day. He wants us to be His peacemakers. We must say nice things when other people say nasty things. We must give with love when other people grab everything. We must offer comfort where other people cause hurt. We must let God's peace run through the whole world like a peaceful stream.

Something to Do

Next time you are going to say goodbye to someone, say "Peace to you" instead. That's what they used to say in Bible times.

Something to Think About

God wants to give you a heart filled with peace.

Prayer

Dear Jesus, please put a river of peace deep within my heart. Amen.

Only Your Best

This is the day the Lord has made.
We will rejoice and be glad in it.
Psalm 118:24

What do you like to do best? Do you like coloring in? Swimming? Baking cupcakes with Mom? Washing the car with Dad? Or building sand castles on the beach?

God wants us to do nice things. He likes it when we are having fun. He wants us to have fun every day. He just wants a "thank You." How do we thank Him? By giving Him our best.

When you color in, it makes God smile when you use all the pretty colors. When you bake cupcakes with Mom, it makes God glad when you decorate them. When you help Dad wash the car, He is proud of every shiny part that you polish yourself. When you build a sand castle, God claps His hands when you build an extra tower just for Him!

When we give our best to God, the most difficult tasks become easy, because we are not alone. God is with us. We are a team. The best team! We can even finish hard work with a smile!

Something to Do

Pick a handful of leaves. Place the leaves in the shape of a heart for Jesus.

Something to Think About

God wants you to do your best for Him.

Prayer

Look, Jesus! I'm doing my very best just for You.

Amen.

I Can Fly!

Those who trust in the Lord
will find new strength. They will
soar high on wings like eagles.
Isaiah 40:31

The eagle is the king of the birds. It is big and strong and brave. That is why you see an eagle on many emblems.

An eagle only needs to flap its wings a few times and voila! He soars through the blue skies. He swishes between the clouds and wiggles in the wind.

The eagle's nest is high up in the mountains. There the chicks are safe. Their friends are the sun and the wind and the rain. And the small animals that share the cliff with them.

The eagle flies far to find food. Sometimes he has to fight for his food. Other times he must fly through a storm.

Something to Do

Keep a feather in your Bible to remind you that God helps you to soar high on wings like eagles!

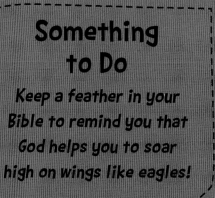

Something to Remember

God wants to give you wings like eagles to soar above any problems.

His two huge wings will never ever fail him. He can always count on them. They always bring him back safely to the nest.

God wants me to be His eagle. He makes me brave and strong. He gives me wings to rise above my problems. When I trust Him, He gives me strength. He will never let me down. I just need to flap my wings. God will help me soar high above the things that scare me.

Prayer

Dear Jesus, thank You for making me soar with wings like an eagle.

Amen.

A Child Is Born

She gave birth to her first
child, a son. She wrapped
Him snugly in strips of cloth
and laid Him in a manger.
Luke 2:7

Mary is home alone. She is washing the dishes and sweeping the floor. Suddenly an angel stands right next to her. Mary gets a fright, but the angel talks with a soft voice. He says, "Do not be afraid. God has a special job for you. You are going to have baby boy. You must call Him Jesus. He will be called the Son of God."

"I cannot have a baby," said Mary. "I am not married!"

"It is going to be a very special Baby," said the angel. "He will be born of the Holy Spirit."

"Then it is good," said Mary.

Not long after that Mary became pregnant. The angel explained everything to Joseph, Mary's fiancé. Joseph was obedient. He married Mary. Together they waited for the Baby to be born.

When it was almost time for the Baby to be born, all the people had to be counted. So Mary and Joseph went to Bethlehem to be counted there. It was a long and difficult journey. The only place that they could find to sleep in Bethlehem was a stable.

That night Baby Jesus was born among the sheep and other animals. And high above in the sky the brightest star could be seen!

Something to Think About

God sent His Son from
heaven to come to earth
to save us.

Something to Do

Ask Mom's help to cut
out a star from shiny
paper. Stick it to the wall
above your bed. Imagine
you are with Joseph
and Mary in the stable.

Prayer

Dear Jesus, thank You
for coming to earth to save us.
Amen.

A Very Special Stone

"I will give to each one a white stone, and on the stone will be engraved a new name that no one understands except the one who receives it."
Revelation 2:17

God loves it when His children obey Him. He wants us to listen to Mom and Dad and our teachers and grandparents and aunts and uncles.

God also wants us to listen to His voice. He does not always talk to you with words. Sometimes it is just a feeling: a "yes feeling" or a "no feeling."

You know the "yes feeling" — you get that feeling when you help Mom with chores in the house.

Or if you give someone a hug. Or if Dad tells you, "Good job!" It is a great feeling. Almost like walking on the clouds!

You probably also know the awful "no feeling" — you get that feeling when you have told a lie. Or when you had a fight with your friend. Or if Mom disciplines you. It is not nice. Then it feels as if your heart is breaking.

God does not want us to do wrong things. He wants us to be obedient and keep ourselves busy with good things.

For everyone who is obedient, God has a surprise. When He returns to earth again, He will give you a white stone, with a brand-new name on it. A special name that only you and God understand.

Something to Think About

God wants us to
be obedient.

Something to Do

Look for a white stone.
Give it to your best friend.
Tell your friend about God's
promise for children
who are obedient.

Prayer

Dear Jesus, I want to be obedient.
Help me to hear Your voice
when You speak to me.
Amen.

Say Sorry When You Are Wrong

"You may freely eat the fruit of every tree in the garden – except the tree of the knowledge of good and evil."

Genesis 2:16-17

Adam and Eve were very happy. They had the whole Garden of Eden to themselves. In the garden the most beautiful trees grew. And they bore the sweetest fruits. Adam and Eve could eat the fruits of all the trees in the garden. There was just one tree in the middle of the garden — they were not to eat from that tree.

One day Adam and Eve were disobedient. They tasted the fruit of the tree in the middle of the garden. God punished them. He told them to leave the garden.

God put an angel at the gate of the garden.
Adam and Eve could never return again.
They were very sorry about what they had done.

We are also sometimes naughty, just like Adam and
Eve. We fight with our friends. We don't listen to Mom.
We take something that does not belong to us.
Such things make God sad.

But God loves us so much that He will never chase
us away.

It is also never too late to say you are sorry. To say
sorry is like a broom that sweeps a floor clean.
It sweeps all the bad things away. We can then
forget about them, because they are gone.

Something to Do

Ask Mom if you can use the broom and sweep the kitchen floor for her. Pretend that the broom sweeps away all the naughty things you have done.

Something to Think About

God wants us to say sorry when we are wrong.

Prayer

Dear Jesus, I am sorry that I am sometimes naughty. Amen.

God's Name Is Holy

"Pray like this: Our Father in heaven,
may Your name be kept holy."
Matthew 6:9

The Bible tells us that it is wrong to say bad words. We must never ever use God's name in a bad way.

Once, Dad was busy in the garage fixing a kitchen chair. He accidentally hit his thumb with the hammer and he said a bad word. I was very cross with him and he immediately said sorry!

God has many names. Most of the time we call Him Jesus, Lord or Holy Spirit. His other names are Father, Emmanuel, and Savior. God's name is holy. It means His name is special. And we must only use His name with respect.

We must look after God's name like a precious treasure. We must not use it in a bad way. When we hurt ourselves or get a fright we mustn't say a swear word. We must only use God's name when we talk about Him and the Bible. And of course when we speak to Him. He likes that very much!

Something to Do

Listen when people talk. Can you hear when they use God's name in the wrong way? You may tell them not to do so – in a nice way, even if it is a grown-up.

Something to Think About

God's name is holy.

Prayer

Dear Jesus, help me to treasure Your name like a precious jewel. Amen.

Rest a Bit

On the seventh day God had finished His work of creation, so He rested from all His work.
Genesis 2:2

God made our wonderful world in six days: On the first day He created light and darkness. On the second day He made the blue skies. On the third day He created the dry land and all the plants. On the fourth day He created the sun, moon and stars. On the fifth day He made the birds and the fish in the sea. On the sixth day He created the wild animals. He left the best for last: people!

God looked at everything. And He was very happy. But He was tired. So on the seventh day He rested.

We are also very busy during the week. Mom and Dad work. We must go to school. Mom prepares dinner for us and Dad helps us with our homework. We all help to do the dishes. Even Buster brings his bowl so we can clean it.

On a Friday Mom bakes a cake. On Saturday Dad washes his car. We do shopping and watch TV.

"Whew, that was nice!" we say.

"Tomorrow is Sunday," says Mom when she kisses us goodnight. "It is God's day. So we will just relax and rest a bit, just like God did long ago."

Something to Do

Turn around and around until you are tired. Lie on the ground and rest a bit until the world stops spinning.

Something to Think About

God wants us to rest on Sundays.

Prayer

Dear Jesus, sometimes I want to play when I need to rest. Help me to remember to rest like You did.

Amen.

The Song of the Tapping Beetle

"Here I am! I stand at the door and knock."
Revelation 3:20

The tapping beetle is lonely. He is looking for a friend. That is why he plays his special song. He does not use a guitar or a flute. He uses his shiny body to make a tapping sound. His song sounds like this: "Tick-tick-tick … tick-tick … come closer, pretty tapping-beetle girl."

The tapping beetle taps the whole night long. Every now and then he stops and listens. He waits for a lady friend to answer him. He will not stop before he finds a mate.

The tapping beetle's hard work is worth it.
When the moon rises behind the bushes, another
tapping beetle answers with her own song: "Tick-tick-
tick ... tick-tick ... I like your song!"

The beetle is glad. He walks fast to find his friend.
Tomorrow the forest insects will come to their wedding.

God is even more patient than a tapping beetle. He knocks
on the doors of our hearts every day: knock-knock ...
knock-knock. He knocks until we open the door.
He never gives up, no matter how long we
take. He wants us to invite Him in to come
and live in our hearts forever.

Something to Do

Ask Mom to knock on the front door. Imagine it is Jesus. Now open the door and say, "Welcome in my heart!"

Something to Think About

God knocks on the door of your heart until you open for Him.

Prayer

Dear Jesus, I open the door of my heart wide for You. Please come in! Amen.

Blow, Wind, Blow!

Every night Dad watches the weather on TV.
The weatherman says the wind is going to blow.
He tells us how strong the wind will blow. And from
which direction. "Will it be a cold southern wind?
Or will it be a warm easterly wind?" we wonder.

"Take your sweater with you to school," Mom says.

Sometimes the wind is just a light breeze. Other times
it is so strong that the trees bend and the clouds are
blown around. No one can tell the wind what to do.

Every now and then the weatherman says it is going to be a beautiful day with no wind. And then the wind creeps up on us and blows everything around.

The Holy Spirit is like the wind. He blows wherever He wants. Today He blows the door of my heart wide open. Tomorrow He blows your heart full of love. The day after that He heals your friend's broken heart. The Holy Spirit even blows forgiveness into the hearts of people who are mad at each other.

There is not one corner where the wind of the Holy Spirit cannot reach!

Something to Think About

The Holy Spirit is like the wind. It blows wherever it wants.

Something to Do

Ask Mom to switch on the fan. Stand in front of the wind. Pretend it is the Holy Spirit blowing over you.

Prayer

Blow, Holy Spirit, blow.
Blow me to where You want me.
Amen.

Shhhhh ...

***After the fire there was
the sound of a gentle whisper.***
1 Kings 19:12

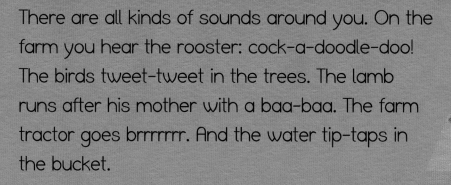

There are all kinds of sounds around you. On the farm you hear the rooster: cock-a-doodle-doo! The birds tweet-tweet in the trees. The lamb runs after his mother with a baa-baa. The farm tractor goes brrrrrrr. And the water tip-taps in the bucket.

The sounds in the city are different. The airplane takes off with a shhhhhhhuuuush. The train goes choo-choo into the station. The cars drive by with a vrooooom. Every now and then you hear a honk-honk.

In our house there are many sounds and noises. The TV, the radio, the phone. The alarmclock wakes us up with a trrrrrrrrr. The microwave stops with a tiiiing. The doorbell goes ding-dong. And in between we talk and laugh together.

God wants a turn to speak in all the noise. He wants us to hear His voice. But we need silence to hear Him. God does not talk with a loud voice. He whispers in a soft voice deep inside our hearts.

God is patient. He waits until you become quiet and nothing can distract you. Then He speaks to you in a way you can understand.

Something to Do

Sit very quietly for a while. Close your eyes and listen. Name three things that you can hear. Is silence one of them?

Something to Think About

God wants you to become quiet so that He can speak to you.

Prayer

Dear Jesus, I am listening. You can whisper to my heart. Amen.

Come to Me

"Come to Me ..."
Matthew 11:28

Aunt Emma walks in her garden. She is looking for the most beautiful rose. The rose must have red petals and be wide open. And it must smell very good. The rose must be the princess of the garden!

Aunt Emma does not even notice the shy daisy hiding behind the tree. The little flower is white and yellow. Her leaves are not so neat. And she does not smell as nice as Princess Rose.

But the daisy is very brave. She turns her head happily towards the sun every day.

We are sometimes like flowers. Some children are Princess Roses. They are pretty, and rich and good at everything. Everyone wants to be their friend.

Other children are like the daisy. We are not as pretty and our clothes are not as new and we cannot run as fast. But we do our best every day.

The Bible has good news for us! To God it does not matter if we are a rose or a daisy. He does not care about how we look on the outside. He also does not care if you come last. He tells you, "You are precious. Come to Me ..."

Something to Do

Call your best friend and invite them over. Tell them about the good news that God is calling all of us to Him.

Something to Think About

God calls us to come to Him.

Prayer

Dear Jesus, here I am.
I belong to You.
Amen.

Be like Salt

"You are the salt of the earth."
Matthew 5:13

Mom likes to cook. In winter she makes soups and stews. In summer she makes jello and custard. When it is my birthday, she bakes me a cake with candles on it! She puts salt in everything she bakes or cooks.

Mom says salt makes her food taste better. Food without salt tastes bland. Salt even makes the chocolate pudding taste better!

God wants us to be salt too. When your friend is sad, you can be the salt and make him or her smile again and feel better. When Grandma is sick, you can sit with her. When friends fight you can help them make up. When someone uses bad words, you can help them stop. God's children can make an ordinary day as nice as chocolate pudding, with a little bit of salt!

Something to Do

Repeat the following tongue twister as fast as you can: Sally's salty seashore shells.

Something to Think About

You must be salt for other people on earth, God's salt.

Prayer

Dear Jesus, I want to cheer others up. Help me to be salt. Amen.